Local News from Someplace Else

Local News from Someplace Else

MARJORIE MADDOX

WIPF & STOCK · Eugene, Oregon

LOCAL NEWS FROM SOMEPLACE ELSE

Copyright © 2013 Marjorie Maddox. All rights reserved. Except for brief quotations in critical publications or reviews, no part of this book may be reproduced in any manner without prior written permission from the publisher. Write: Permissions, Wipf and Stock Publishers, 199 W. 8th Ave., Suite 3, Eugene, OR 97401.

Wipf & Stock
An Imprint of Wipf and Stock Publishers
199 W. 8th Ave., Suite 3
Eugene, OR 97401

www.wipfandstock.com

ISBN 13: 978-1-62564-094-9

Manufactured in the U.S.A.

Dedication
To Gary, my safe haven

Contents

Acknowledgments | **xi**

Section I

The Postcard | **3**
Homecoming | **5**
Housed | **6**
Treat | **7**
Sixteen-Inch Black-and-White | **8**
Local News from Someplace Else | **9**
Best Friend | **11**
Safe | **12**
Fifth-Grader Imagined Taking over School | **13**
The Good Mother Hides from Photographers | **14**
Musca Domestica | **16**
Pennsylvania September: The Witnesses | **17**
Later | **21**
Nine Alive! | **23**
Backwards Barn Raising | **24**
June 1st Liturgy | **25**
Seven-Year-Old Girl Escapes from Kidnappers | **27**
Fatal Shock Mystery: Experts Look for Answers after Tragedy | **28**

Section II

July Foothills: | **33**

Anachronism | **34**

Cancer Diagnosis | **35**

Meteorology | **37**

Anniversary Coffee | **38**

Minersville Diner | **39**

After | **41**

Sea Side Be | **42**

Renting | **43**

Frequent Flyer Miles | **44**

Extra Towels | **45**

Photographing the Spa for the Color Brochure | **46**

Learning to Weather | **47**

Real Estate Sign | **48**

First Night in a New Place | **49**

Ithaca Winter | **50**

First Snow | **51**

Conversion | **52**

Woman, 91, Frozen to Floor | **53**

Montoursville, PA | **55**

Jazz Memorial | **56**

Death-Defying | **57**

Gluttony | **58**

Reoccurring Storms | **59**

Twice | **61**

Section III

39 | **65**

In the Pearle Vision Center Waiting Room | **66**

Clyde Peeling's Reptiland | **68**

Indelible | **70**

At the Gynecologist's | **72**

Plea to an Embryo | **73**

Donation | **74**

First Layout | **75**

Twin Infants at the Olan Mills Portrait Studio | **76**

Swimming Pregnant at the YWCA | **77**

March 16 | **78**

Afternoon Nap | **79**

The Time Is Midnight | **80**

Appropriate | **81**

Mona Lisa | **83**

Abstract | **84**

Goldfish | **85**

H. G. Who? | **87**

Still Life of House in Late March | **88**

Settled | **89**

After Having Children, We Reintroduce Ourselves to Bicycles | **91**

A. M. : Inside and Out | **92**

Acknowledgments

The author gratefully acknowledges the following publications in which many of the poems first appeared.

Adanna: "After Having Children, We Reintroduce Ourselves to Bicycles," "Goldfish"

American Jones Building & Maintenance. Ed. Von G. Binuia. Concord, NH: Missing Spoke Press, 1999: "Settled," "Still Life of House in Late March"

Arabesques: "Extra Towels," "First Snow"

BigCityLit: "Photographing the Spa for the Color Brochure"

Blackwater Review: "Gluttony"

Blueline: "Ithaca Winter"

Boxcar Poetry Review: "Appropriate"

Christianity & Literature: "June 1st Liturgy," "Minersville Diner," "Still Life of House in Late March"

Common Wealth: Contemporary Poets on Pennsylvania. Eds. Marjorie Maddox and Jerry Wemple. State College, PA: Penn State University Press, 2005: "Pennsylvania September: The Witnesses"

Drexel On-Line: "Appropriate"

Drive, She Said: "Renting"

Essential Love. Ed. Ginny Lowe Connors. West Hartford, CN: Poetworks/Grayson Books, 2000: "The Time Is Midnight"

Fiddleblack: "Real Estate Sign"

The Heart of All That Is: Reflections on Home. Ed. Jim Perlman. Duluth, MN: Holy Cow! Press, 2013: "Settled"

Acknowledgments

Hurricane Blues: Poems about Katrina and Rita. Eds. Philip C. Kolin and Susan Swartwout. Cape Girardeau, MO: Southeast Missouri State University Press, 2006: "Jazz Memorial"

In a Fine Frenzy: Poets Respond to Shakespeare. Eds. David Starkey and Paul J. Willis. Iowa City: University of Iowa Press, 2005: "Cancer Diagnosis"

Inkwell: "Montoursville, PA"

Inspirit: "Pennsylvania September: The Witnesses"

Literary Mama: "Afternoon Nap"

Martin Luther King, Jr. Project: "Woman, 91, Frozen to Floor"

The Mom Egg: "First Layout"

The Montserrat Review: "Indelible"

New Verse News: "Reoccurring Storms"

North Carolina Humanities Review: "Conversion"

North Chicago Review: "Woman, 91, Frozen to Floor"

The Other Journal: "Nine Alive!"

Petroglyph: "Learning to Weather"

phati'tude Literary Magazine: "Jazz Memorial"

Reconfigurations: "Abstract"

Remembering the Future. Eds. Chris Keller and Andrew David. Eugene, OR: Cascade Books, 2008: "Nine Alive!"

Runes: "Death Defying," 2004 Finalist for Runes Poetry Award, judged by Jane Hirschfield

The Same: "Anachronism," "Backwards Barn Raising," "H. G. Who?" "Homecoming"

Say the Word: Poems on Joy, 2002 Contest Finalist, judged by David St. John: "Extra Towels"

So to Speak: "Twin Infants at the Olan Mills Portrait Studio"

Standing on the Ceiling. Ed. and Illus. Joanne Fox. Sausalito, CA: Foxfold Press, 1998: "Afternoon Nap," "Treat"

Thin Air: "Donation"

Verse Wisconsin: "Fatal Shock Mystery: Experts Look for Answers after Tragedy"

Watershed: "Montoursville, PA"

The Women's Review of Books: "39," "Swimming Pregnant at the YWCA," "Woman, 91, Frozen to Floor"

Section I

THE POSTCARD

> Summer is going quickly. We are
> very busy. My brother and his family all
> died in a plane crash. Hope to see
> you soon when we fly that way . . .

What we scrunch on a 3 x 5
wants happiness as bland
as the heat waving at us
from beneath its sunglasses and umbrella,
simplicity so boring we relax in it,
order another drink.

But somewhere between
the Eiffel Tower and Empire State Building,
between your miss you's and wish you were here's,
fact slips in, inked lightning across skies
as bright as a Las Vegas smile.

In a postcard of Sunset Strip
amidst a list of Hollywood celebrities:
"The plane was the same
as JFK, jr.'s." And on the backside
of the Tomb of the Unknown Soldier:
"The memorial service was short."

All summer I listen
for clouds cracking open with you,
your brief alphabet of grief swooping in
from the skies with the late-morning mail.

There is room here to land
in the ordinary,
a clearing for what is missing.

I'm waiting to hear from Madrid,
from Tokyo and Madagascar,
where loss, I've read, flies fastest
in the smallest of words.

HOMECOMING

And maybe when you arrive—
stumbling up the cracked path
thick with hopscotch chalk and weeds—
a stranger will answer the door,
insist you're no longer on Elm,
that this is not your home.

Autumn will well up, swell in the gutters
you cleaned every year since twelve,
spill into the color of a landscape
you can't see but feel,
bricks untwining, ivy crumbling,
smoke unbraiding from clouds.

Maybe then you will turn
away from the echo of a knock
back into your own life,
away from my picket-fence memory,
framed still in this dilapidated doorway,
wondering who you are.

HOUSED

The day we were to look for houses,
wide with porches and promised sun, houses creaking

with our middle-age bones in rockers; with shutters
stretched open to your upcoming cries and staccato coos;

houses brimming with your grins and girly muses
singing nursery-land tunes in our sleep, our sleep,

that day you, a backwards burglar in my body's house, broke out
in black water, too soon, too soon,

sounded the alarm till Emergency came running
to cuff you off to breath and barred hospital cribs.

But first you had to live and wouldn't cooperate.
The authorities took you in hand, called in the helicopters

to whir you over uneven rows of un-owned homes
which we, the expectant buyers, didn't see,

didn't see, because in your rebellious escape
and capture into our lives, you were born,

were born, robber of our once-empty dwellings,
thief of our well-housed affections.

TREAT

Shadows bloom and wilt across the patio,
our new home sheds flakes of bright paint,
and, of course, it is October; the neighbors we don't know
hang pumpkin lights like lamb's blood over the threshold,
and from their porch rocking chairs stare at us, the strangers.

We disguise ourselves with smiles and wave.
And why not? Let the leaves fall and the grass grow high,
our new life floats around us in the frost-free air,
and we own the chaos of autumn; the weeds
would grow between our toes if we'd linger

into another two seasons. We are giddy enough
for a picket fence or a pink flamingo
and bring out Baby to see the splendor.
"Here," we say like good parents, "is the color red
and over there, the irrepressible orange of joy."

SIXTEEN-INCH BLACK-AND-WHITE

    square   portal
    of space   to Space,
    that grainy,   last frontier
    now front   and center,
    armchair   and moon
       close   companions.

Beyond camera and crew; beyond Houston; beyond airwaves that ride high outside our knowledge; beyond Mrs. Stouffer's mashed potatoes, every mother, father, sister, brother huddled about a set, those grounded rabbit ears tuning us into a future beyond that edge-of-our-seats shot filmed 'round the world; beyond all that—we're there, each of us, two-stepping between craters, bouncing into wild blue possibility far beyond 1969 and our three-channel, living-room imagination, desperately dreaming of soaring beyond what we already know of beyond.

LOCAL NEWS FROM SOMEPLACE ELSE

It's still sci-fi,
this slim disk catching sky in its curve,
luring invisible signals.

Unsightly aliens,
satellite dishes dot suburban lawns,
click code into unsuspecting homes.

Here is not anywhere close
to captions crossing television screens,
unconvincingly disguising our town

as Tulsa or Tuscaloosa
where the same two masked men
stick up a shiny gas station,

smile suspiciously into the eye
of the security camera.
Perhaps they are you

or your cousins traveling through
another state or time
into this 27-inch space

of otherworldliness, the familiar
and foreign switching uniforms
to the tune of Time and Temperature.

It is always snowing or raining
someplace like here
while our own windows lie

their pretend sunshine
on a street somewhat like yours.
Whom can we trust

when a smiling anchor
prophesies the utmost danger
around the corner

of tomorrow? Today, someone's
floods will rise up
past the screen, our remote a small boat

of numbers, helpless with no
SOS in the making.
Brushfires will spark from antennae

hunching too close to our house
while hurricanes huff through wires.
We try to look outside

to our own doings, but all fingers
are frozen. No matter
what channel we pay,

there is still no news from home.

BEST FRIEND

> Hound Shoots Croatian Hunter
> —Newspaper Headline; *Jutarnji List Daily*, 10/04

I could have told you, Spaso Ivosevic,
this is the way of all clichés on friendship.
If not your back, then your ankle,
the bullet path centimeters outside
your peripheral vision,
the pain, yes, unexpected, but as inevitable
as the woods' lure, the joy
of the kill.

You'll live but with a limp,
if you're lucky, a scar
large enough to warn others,
yourself.

Sure, you tell me he was chasing
chickens, stormed past, for just a second,
turned those puppy eyes
on something else. Such loyalty,
you'd hate to put him down. What does it matter—
gun propped against the wall,
you, a veteran? I've heard it before,

typed up the medical reports
seconds before that other gunshot,
the one aimed for the head.

SAFE

My baby and I stay home
from the funeral for the murdered child,
unrecognizably battered and stabbed
in last week's news photos.

The police arrive early
at the church, the estranged wife
and husband, separated by rows of pews,
glare at photographers, suspect
each other. They have both

aimed guns. My husband lights
church candles around the girl's enlarged
classroom photo, prays
for us. What is safe lurks

nowhere near, doubt encrypting
fear, the way we cross
ourselves in our cloistered home.

We stare nightly at neighbors
walking too close to the nursery window,
too close to the woods
where the girl was found,

her arms criss-crossed just so
as if by a parent who can
no longer sleep.

FIFTH-GRADER IMAGINED TAKING OVER SCHOOL

>   –Newspaper Headline; Wellsboro, PA

All the safe, small towns—
gas streetlights silly in retrospect—
proclaim surprise. What else
when their children's open
veins stain the school tiles?
*Here the cornstalks stay calm;
the cost-of-living low?*

The cobblestone streets empty out
from all but spectators shooting cameras,
murder and media sole companions
in this former tourist-attraction for tranquility.

Eventually, summer skateboarders
will again hunt back roads,
barefoot teens will dive
into abandoned swimming holes,
grade-schoolers at bat will boast
that they were there, that day,
in the hallway, the cafeteria,
the next classroom over.

On the hottest day
when a small town's boredom sizzles
into the limbs of its children,
they will wonder what it was like to aim,
to hit the target fast and accurately,
to explode in the unfamiliar dazzle
of forbidden city lights.

THE GOOD MOTHER HIDES FROM PHOTOGRAPHERS

All week they've stolen her daughter's face,
rolled it up, delivered it in late editions
to each waiting neighbor, all of whom
are quoted passionately as saying,
"She comes from a good family.
We don't understand."

Neither does she, hiding behind
her just-washed curtains,
the family portraits eyeing her disgrace.
Reporters ring the bell,
wait for her good manners
to reclaim her.

It is time for school,
her daughter appropriately housed
behind evenly spaced bars,
her unsure lips as complex as fingerprints.
Even this is a photographic exhibit
with the wrong captions.

Behind her 8 x 10 door,
the good mother develops
polite excuses, snaps
small portraits of her family's past
with her black-and-white eyes,
pastes them behind the present.
She has forgotten how to pose,
where to focus her attention.

In that other studio,
her daughter will cry
without her,
her young silhouette striking
and beautiful even there,
her eyes negatives of what was.

Meanwhile, on the front porch
the photographers raise
their lenses, adjust their stares.
Soon, the good mother will
open the door, look away toward the edge
of the frame—there,
where she needs to step
out of the picture.

MUSCA DOMESTICA

> God made nothing without a purpose.
> But the fly comes close.
> –Mark Twain

You of the aerobatic patterns,
unpredictable even to self,
you crave our waste

and we fly after you,
zigzag across your air
with webbed swats

to protect what we do not want.
What power in your pads,
transporting microorganisms cost-free,

colonies slaughtered with a buzz.
We envy your place on the ceiling
but won't relent.

Twitching at the sight
of your wings, we suck in
with our own proboscis.

What soars between
your antennae steers us.

With your aviator eyes,
you see who we are.

PENNSYLVANIA SEPTEMBER: THE WITNESSES

UNITED AIRLINES FLIGHT 93

Allegheny County Emergency Coordinator

Something made it pivot,
duck its nose at Cleveland and turn
away from San Francisco and the mounting sun
unabashedly displaying its ordinary face.

Nineteen times that Ohio Center called out
for contact, safety, confirmation, any
answer to the circling back over the Keystone,
over the routine of our lives,
all that came before.

Controllers and pilots, we all listened
for the practiced SOS,
then translated to fear that static
of turmoil, cockpit havoc,
radio mistaken for intercom,
the unplanned for and unfamiliar
voice commandeering crew
and passengers toward calm, those strangers
now confidently on their way towards Pittsburgh,
boasting a bomb.

Westmoreland County 911 Dispatcher

Almost 10:00 a.m. and his voice escaped
that locked bathroom, that 757 diving
toward disaster, loss of hope and altitude
infiltrating the airwaves of our county,
our headquarters, my desk.

His name, he said, was Edward Felt.
The plane, he said, was hijacked,
and all the mapped-out EMS routes
clicked on full-force in the circuitry
of my sleep-deprived brain and took off
into air over the farm houses of those I'd helped save;
over the chipped-paint homes of those we found too late,
unable to survive any siren-escorted stretcher,
their family's prayers wailing past clouds
only to firework into flame.

The Cell Phones

After the first shock of TV news,
we were the 21st-century messengers
of still more, our coiled cells crackling out confusion
across Somerset county to both coasts.

Drafted, conduits of chaos and courage,
we assisted duty, the fear beneath:
unrehearsed confessions, the 23rd Psalm,
I love you's saved on answering machine tapes,
last minutes of bravery rewound and replayed
after that unanimous *No!* filled the fields
and abandoned mines of Pennsylvania
with lonely awe.

The wind was echoing.

Auto Service Station Owner, Shanksville

Turns out we were 'bout three miles down
but, I swear, it coulda been the next block.

Shook the whole station.
Some people's windows blasted open,
like it was the furnace or something.

"Two loud bangs, then straight down,"
some gal over the hill told me later.
And a high-pitched screech—that too.

Of course, we alls ran outside,
that fire whistle blowing
something fierce.

The Bike Riders

A twirling fireball,
that engine gunned twice,
house windows rattling all around,
then smoke rising right up
signal-style from below the tree line.

When we got there:
the whole damn field on fire,
trees plowed down and this big hole—
broad as a barn and deep—
uninvited in the ground.

The First Photographer

I grabbed my camera quick-like,
tracked that smoke
to a few acres of grass and weeds
below the old strip mine.

I clicked automatically,
focusing pain.

In the trees, what was left
of metal and flesh.
Beyond the woods, the scorched crater
swallowing who I was.

I Watch a Mother at the Year Memorial

Even now, the hills lie
too beautifully below sky,
fabricate disbelief.
How can the wrens sing?

Piles of trinkets collapse
beneath new flags and plastic tulips,
messages scrawled to the dead
on portable toilets,
guardrails of makeshift parking lots.

"Such an ugly thing to happen
in this lovely place," she said,
turning to leave.

LATER

At fourteen, my daughter
can't recall Harris and Klebold,
cafeterias mangled by massacre.
The pick of victims, the pitch of fear,
the clicks of semiautomatics all trigger nothing
in her post-Columbine brain.

She was two, just walking
into this world of wonder
gone wrong. By four, she'd toppled
tower after tower of blocks;
finger-painted the nation's bright tragedy;
watched as those older than she
collected jagged shards of disaster.

Aftermath is a vocabulary word
she learned early,
before prehistoric jargon
for what she couldn't understand
or already knew too well.

At fourteen, my daughter knows
each brick of her school but can't recall
Elizabeth, who—tired of bullies—aimed and fired
six months before 9/11, two days after
the slaughter at Santana High.
She was fourteen, the uniforms and cafeteria
the same. That time, nobody died.

Youth ages with anger, contradictions
the fad. What we know or
don't merges into unknown quantities
only partly erased from blackboards
long ago replaced by YouTube depictions of history.

The Surgeon General has confirmed
polished apples are unsafe for teachers.
Gift cards to the mall remain
an acceptable alternative—
unless it's a mall near Columbine.

Which lessons heal?
Which blast open old wounds?
At fourteen. My daughter.

NINE ALIVE!

> –Newspaper headline; Somerset, PA

This is the popular miracle
we bow down to,
a gasp in the throats of thousands
ready to weep,
disbelief finally synonymous with relief
and not that dark mine of tragedy
that keeps collapsing
around this tunnel of a country.

But there are other wonders, too,
untelevised, deeper down,
the tap-tap-tapping
of what is left of our breath
hungry for spirit—
that canary not yet dead
in our damp labyrinth—
the way we long for light,
for even a candle-glow of rejoicing
for what was once lost;
"Alive! Still Alive!"
our pulse mutters,
trying to pray.

BACKWARDS BARN RAISING

Nickel Mines, October 2006

And what can we do but wail with you,
grief burning back to ashes

those splintered schoolroom boards
that heard the bullets?

Flames hot enough to melt the nails—
now and then—

rise up in our eyes; we hear
that ancient hammer thud

echo, "*Eli, Eli,
lama sabachthani?*"

Can what is lost be leveled?
You hold each others' hands,

huddle in an unending circle,
". . . . as we forgive those who trespass against us."

Even out of this,
you build forgiveness.

JUNE 1ST LITURGY

In the ordinariness of a day
bright with just-because,
we salivate, swill Bud, chew well-done
chops slaughtered last week
by your brother-in-law.

Earlier, you made
Bach bellow through pipes,
pumped the organ beyond the ordinary
stone walls of the nearby resort chapel.
You do not believe the truth
of our praise.

The retired priest believes
the words of your hymns, hums them
into his sermon, stretches truth
across a congregation chewing the Ordinary.

Over barbecue,
you stretch his life across a lawn
that praises the ordinary,
your words drained of rhythm
but bright with what we slaughter.

At his retirement party,
his first wife believed
it was a closet, stepped in,
two flights of stairs bellowing
their rhythm across her spine and neck.
What could she hum on the way down
but hell, the bright dark of death praising
the ordinariness of error?

He remarried an ordinary
parishioner, believed the bright hope
of youth could bellow rhythms
drained from his faithful throat.
She feeds him creamed beef,
hums him to sleep with hymns
she wants to believe.

We stare at the green beans
and weeds in your garden,
devour the rhubarb cobbler
your wife feeds us.

As a child, you played "Funeral Director,"
dreamed of orchestrating
the ordinariness of death;
instead you pedal hymns
and belief at summer resorts.

We believe everything
in all its extraordinary rhythms,
hum a liturgy between Buds
composed from your leftover Bach.

SEVEN-YEAR-OLD GIRL ESCAPES FROM KIDNAPPERS

—Newspaper headline, 8/02

And we climb with her
out of that abandoned basement
through the now-broken window,
her mouth and wrists a raw witness
of what she clawed through,
a temper tantrum to reclaim her life.

Or maybe we're the others
in this neighborhood of gang executions,
tugging her up and out
into a city not brotherly,
a ghost-world of gray,
a village of others

not found or found
too late, over a ridge
in the lying light of dawn
where someone not us
will touch the remains,
decipher the bones,
mouth the fragile names
of those so recently young
in a people gone old.

FATAL SHOCK MYSTERY:
EXPERTS LOOK FOR ANSWERS AFTER TRAGEDY

–Newspaper Headline; *The Columbus Dispatch*

As always, *how* is the question,
superstition trailing. A child, again,
but this time the mystery is more
physical. Or just as.
                In my hometown,
after he oohed and aahed through
my favorite childhood museum,
each questionable atom explained
with tangible scientific exhibits,
molecules lining up to tempt the mind,
recharge adolescence with queries,
                the boy and his friend
scampered home simply like a boy and his friend,
unaware of gravity's pull, of what sparks
our fires, sends the current within
and through.
                The city shrugs its shoulders,
confused by the lack of evidence, except the body
electrocuted on the bridge beside the lamppost.
But let's back up to the boys pitching stones,
trying to squeeze through chain link,
with nothing there suggesting God's
premeditation.

                    Not even the scientific
explanation to fall back on or crawl through,
just the body after the jolt
with no hope of knowing *where*
it came from. The unknown *why*
is expected, something
we've been through before.

Section II

JULY FOOTHILLS:

where eye leans
its tired gaze along
the branch-and-bush blur almost
a mountain. It is hot here, the haze
hovers like smoke signs hoping
for help. What can the eye answer,
so small on the other side? The valley's
shallow voice shriveled below?
Over the edge of hill the view comes:
the lying promise of night.

ANACHRONISM

The air chock-full of August
and death is nowhere near suburbia,
showers off, kitchen knives in place,
the spikes of fences boringly dull,
no black-clad teens filming
homemade horror flicks in back alleys;
the blacktop heating up without incident
or accident, and now three small children step out
from the two-story brick on the corner;
their dark hooded capes catching the slight breeze;
their young faces shadow-hidden as they wave
the long silver of their scythes,
twirl twice in their costumes,
then skip down the cracked sidewalk,
confident and knowing. I do not
go after them.

CANCER DIAGNOSIS

I. *O*

Words cage heart and breath,
irregular in trepidation.
Where are the open arms of hope?
This oval of prognostication
clamps prayer, interrogates pulse.
Even a howl echoes
within its ribs.

II. *that this too too sullied flesh*

Skin-deep and rank,
righteousness flees these organs
ripe with mortality's regret.
Wishes are hollow bones.
Even a Faustian switch
cannot remix the obvious.

III. *would melt, thaw*

Soon disease dissolves all self,
liquidates the I.
Listen for the drip of solitude
and relent. The dark waters
of doubt ebb and flow too quickly
downstream.

IV. *and resolve itself into a dew*

Not dust, but drops
about to evaporate in sun,
to rise in the heat of forgiveness,
this strange healing that peels
skin from soul, sanctifying what rots
and is rotten in the state
of who we are.

METEOROLOGY

All day the skies pour, then threaten, then pour again,
making good their promise of gloom,

a comfort really, that what looms eventually crashes down,
rains itself out, or not completely, intent on furthering

its pessimistic forecasts.
Still, there's relief in reliability,

that what each cloud coughs up
gathers and builds on the eyes' horizon,

expectations deepening
with each darkening hue.

And so I crave even the low rumbling
of our longest-forming sorrows,

the truths of all predictions moving past
updraft to downburst to calm.

ANNIVERSARY COFFEE

On this side of plate glass,
the Pennsylvania sky threatens

no one, calms us with what we aren't,
such perfect summer squall the calm

we love in morning
coffee and split croissant.

Those behind the counter
know us and know

when to save what we want,
can order for us, smile at how we smile

at each other's drenched winsomeness. You are
not what I ordered but what I order now

across the café table, across the morning
spread with such delectable savor.

MINERSVILLE DINER

The sign dangles from rusted chains,
denies history with white-wash:
Steve &   Family Restaurant.
Her name—Rosie—is the shadow beneath absence,
like the almost etched-off letters on plate glass
through which we look for answers
in could-be ancestors sopping up time-
tried gravy with biscuits
beneath these coal-scraped hills.

En route to somewhere else,
we stifle laughs, glad for any
conversation, for even questionable
speculation on someone
else's grief, another's suffocating
gossip, not our dust of who-walked-out-on-whom,
not our abandoned mines of what is worse
than flipping fried eggs alone:
already 80 degrees at 8:00 a.m.,
more heat coming up the cracked sidewalk
to greet us.

Without the planned gaps,
there'd be a hundred tiny fractures
in concrete, breaking more
than mothers' backs. We stay
in the blank squares of sidewalk
on the outside of this diner's plate glass,
head toward the Frank 'N Burger,
the Ye Olde Bakery, "Coming Soon!,"
the blue dome of the church,

its painted gold stars winking knowingly
as we pass into the life we pretend is safe
from explosion, from unexpected
and total collapse.

AFTER

Listen. You're breathing
again. The wind flip-flopped past
your chin, leapt off your tongue,
dove head-first toward the lungs
that heaved with the breeze.
This in-and-out is pretty easy
once you have the will.
Oxygen ought to be illegal,
it flies your insides so high
and spins the sky in your eyes.
Look, the horizon is even
and waiting; it's time
to get living again.

SEA SIDE BE

Salt seasons all,
sautés our other lives out,
sun-grills sandy leisure
into each strand of hair,
each sea-stained square
of skin stretched tightly
toward that ungainly octopus
of sun. Listen. The tide's wet breath
wants only you. Let be.

RENTING

Who wouldn't choose
the just-washed white of this Aspire
scripted with eighteen small
miles on a speedometer
that flips its lottery digits
beside the accordion-stretched map
we play into each added-bonus
state of our prize-winning
itinerary?

All hail Economy
and her deceptively large
leg room, her exceptionally parked
body, her 35-miles-per-gallon city-sipping
Vroom-Vroom-Vroom!

Bless her undented fenders,
her souvenir-proportioned trunk.
We are old and in love
with the non-leather seats,
windshield wipers that work
up a beat, doors that open each time
to AAA approval.

If we drive long enough
across this uncalculated country,
how can she not follow us home?
How can she not, remembering
the miles of our affection,
forget how little we paid?

FREQUENT FLYER MILES

land us here,
chewing gum to keep the inner drums
from doubling over. Yes, we know the price
we pay for turbulence but cannot help but holler
in happiness. Look! The air surfs beneath us, down there
with offices and appointments, with all but the few faxes
stowed away here on the backs of seats. Our laptops
have run away to the overhead and it could almost be
the sixties the way we crave Tang,
the way those GQ stewards twist
their demonstration seat belts
into a secret-coded
necklace of love.

EXTRA TOWELS

are what we want,
thick as the blisters
stacked beneath our sneakers.

And newspapers
sprawled provocatively across clean sheets.

Give us beer
for the can opener in the bathroom,
gossip for the in-room fax,
touch-tone fingers for the hundred-plus
channels of cable
deliciously at our command.

Let every tour
dine in castles without us,
dance the pre-paid waltz
beside the postcard Danube.

We are in love
with room service at midnight,
with miniature soaps, whirlpools,
eternal hot water, the overwhelming,
seductive allure of terry.

PHOTOGRAPHING THE SPA FOR THE COLOR BROCHURE

Without us, it is ugly:
waterfall encased in gray
siding, man-made cascades
before calves submerge
to denial. The photographer stages
his display of mums, amber towels,
a plump pumpkin for October's brisk
promise of nature tumbling
into bubbling obedience. Then more
tricks: ladders, extension cords, extra lighting.
FLASH he's transformed summer
patio furniture into cozy
conversational nooks complete with hot
chocolate and toddies; the promised comfort
of terry-cloth. Of course, heat rises
into mist and mystery,
to the still shot that sometime soon
will sell our fabricated lives to suburbanites
who add muscles and limbs,
ordinary torsos, finally
completing the picture
that waits, a little impatiently,
to develop.

LEARNING TO WEATHER

The day after the geese leave,
everything v's in their direction:
angle of voice, sharp line smeared to mascara,
your face a blur of sky wrung out and drying.
It's a change, like weather; you smell it,
stretch out your bones, suspect everything.
To protect you from this, you sing the clipped cry of geese,
stitch to your throat their half-screams.
By mid-spring, as if you and the season were real,
you'll squawk and flutter and flee.

REAL ESTATE SIGN

This is the place unpunctuated with fence posts
and tattered billboards, a brushstroke of sky,
an overly optimistic horizon. Or this is
the place, tyrannical with towers knee-deep
in the institution of county of this is
the place where border crossings collapse
into cascades of well-meaning, meaning
this is the place to drive to
to drive around, sighing, "Potential! Potential!"
before citing overstepped property lines,
trespassing weeds unable to distinguish "place"
from "this is." The place
where unplanted pear trees
preach themselves into perfection. Is it?
The one plot of promised land un-tilled
at the back of your brain? Is it? Quick,
the wind is changing.
The place?

FIRST NIGHT IN A NEW PLACE

The city twitches:
neon and headlight
splotch across this bare apartment,
push the last tone of twilight
until lavender drums
indigo and dusk delivers
herself to the dark
space between note
and note, Thelonious
slipping his dissonance
through the one outlet
the radio reaches
till his keys splinter into static
across an unfinished floor
and what is *alone* is only
and ever.

ITHACA WINTER

To undo who I was, I opened
my chapped lips and swallowed
the weather whole.

Wind chatters grief discriminately,
clicks with the crick in a neck,
the chill in a spine, unzips
eventually what isn't.

Snow fills an eye's iris,
wets the slick of winter,
warms what is without
insides, retrospect burning
its last embers in the grate.

What better white
to white-out absence,
lose the clean slate entirely?

I had a life disappear once.
I stepped out of it into the snow
stacked up like an isosceles triangle
on Seneca Street, an old name and sorrow
stuck at the bottom in a drift.

When I stopped shivering,
behind my teeth were words.

FIRST SNOW

So provisional, it almost doesn't
count—uncourageous, afraid
of everything concrete, the frozen closes in
on asphalt, then vanishes
into nostalgia.

In the streetlight, the sky is all dust,
pale and full of flutter;
on the ground, damp pockets of no longer.

Tentative as first snow reluctant to land,
we move again toward the other,
remember the chill,
the pleasure of complete cover.

CONVERSION

That throaty lure, new ice, invites us
to belief. Both prism and prison, its shards
brighten and bar the underneath,
what glimmers and swims within
the motion we move toward.
It is the oldest action
that swells these atoms, stretches the still
cold; the oldest ardor that holds
us to the land and sails us off. What is not
the river or sea or sand-flattened bottom
converts us into footsteps
across such windowed surfaces
stained suspiciously with cracks.

WOMAN, 91, FROZEN TO FLOOR

It is, after all, Chicago.
Snow is the new mob
ganging up on the elements,
inciting cover-up.

There are innocents,
of course, adrift
in the flurry, caught
white-handed in the cold blast.

The wrong place and time
are where you've always been
in the wrong neighborhood
if you're old and even the blankets

are as frozen as stiff ground
above a coffin. The nice weatherman
accuses, "The streets aren't safe!"
and she locks the doors, double-bolt.

That doesn't stop the break-in,
pipes as brittle as her
wish bones drying on a shelf.
She's hoping for hope,

kneeling now by the pot-belly stove
gone out. But the cold steals in
anyway, shattering steel.
She is soon surrounded

by water, then ice an inch thick.
It muscles about the room,
bullies her, pins her knees
to the slick floor.

You could draw chalk lines
in the air around her,
but it's clumsy with gloves
and she's still moving

her lips. Patrolman
Sadowski translates,
"It's in the frost-
bitten hands of God."

Or maybe just the ice
that lingers on, hunched over
her bare words in that dead room
on the near West Side.

When she's hauled off
for further questioning,
even the ambulance lights
shiver in thick cold.

MONTOURSVILLE, PA

TWA Flight 800

After the blizzards and floods, we weather
not well into this, natural detached
from disaster too explosively to listen
to anything but the hiss of absence.

We throw shadows on a sky
swooping now with sunny indifference,
clouds in the shape of confetti in the shape of airplane
bits and shrapnel. We cannot think

about the neighbors' children,
but the river floats by anyway with its grief
drenched in their laughter, in their jagged joy
of travel soaring full-speed into the blue of possibility.

Meanwhile, the Atlantic clogs
with would-be's, a fisherman pulls in
the memories we want
consummated another day:

a Polaroid shot of boarding the plane,
a dog-eared anthology of poetry,
a postcard of the JFK airport
before everything took off.

JAZZ MEMORIAL

    FOR R. P.

While the band jams,
        your widow passes out
beads as bright as grief.
    I tap my feet
           to "When the Saints . . ."
              and count blessings
      drowned and decayed
                even here, a year after.
You wanted a celebration,
        but I'm stuck in this mud
of memory with my voice
      too moldy to shiver
          to the beat
              of what you didn't believe
      though everyone else is singing
                your syncopated Orleans,
        raising up the dead,
this city's misery out on the streets
              unable to miss a parade.

DEATH-DEFYING

From her husband's teeth, the thin lady hangs,
her star-painted seat twirling as he swings
precariously from his brother's arms,
who dangles upside down, as if harm
knows nothing of the circus wire, taut
between belief and fear. The locals taught
respect for gravity, for faith, for all
that brings the dollars in when crops won't sell.

The larger tale looms outside the tent,
beyond the dried-up field its farmer rents
to last-ditch auctions, hawkers, traveling shows
that feed your hungry kids when corn won't grow.
The sky is blood-black on its outer rim.
The clouds contort and flip; the crowds within,
know nothing of the funnel—or the rain.
The big top twirls closer, juggling pain.

GLUTTONY

In the Wake of Hurricane Sandy

Wood hungry for wood, an oak as large
as ours bites the neighbor's
porch, gutter and screen dangling,
caught in the toothy limbs.

Inverted etiquette, rain washes
the splinters down *before* the meal.
Exhausted from the spread, leaves collapse
all over our yard, dragging their twigs with them.

Even the neighbor's uprooted trunk,
massive and Medusa-like,
passes out on their front lawn, a bad drunk
still sneering at us, the uninvited guests.

REOCCURRING STORMS

> Searchers Find Body of Killed Child in Oklahoma Tornado
> —Associated Press; May 26, 2011
> Mother, 3 Children, Drown in Minivan
> —New York Times; April 14, 2011

Wind/Water, Oklahoma/New York,
the domestically symbolic bathtub/minivan,
two mothers.

And so fear gathers speed, swirls in
or out, grabbing—in its selfish velocity—each state
of who we are or were, what's left
of our man-made lives holding tightly to the already-
born, the life still coming.

Temporarily wedged between faith and scream,
a mother sings reassurances as each
tree, board, sink, tub, life
twists and spins into the horizon
no one foresaw, grief beyond the boundaries
of such predictions, life splintered limb by limb,
like and not like (half a country away)

that other dream-turned-disaster:
depression's dark tunnel twirling
beyond the imaginable, tires whirring
too quickly toward the Hudson,
fueling the speed of no-return,
a family's last vision of sky flooded
with the damp wet of despair.

Except ten-year-old Lashaun,
who—between death and breath—
rolled down his window to let out fear,
then swam toward light.

And in Oklahoma, five-year-old Cathleen,
who, amidst the hurricane's howl,
recognized hope in the heartbeat
of her unborn sibling:
that faint hum in the ear,
or that sudden surge toward possibility

into what one day even you and I—
after a particularly hard day of the ordinary—
might discuss as casually
as weather, as someone else's life.

TWICE

Surveying damage,
calculating costs, he forgot

risks, adhering to the cliché of the unlikely
"like getting struck by. . . ." and went out

with his wife and children watching
into the jagged storm, the split tree

spread-eagle above him like a Frost poem
wounded. And that made all the difference.

Even the careful, wallflower neighbors jumped
when the bolt aimed, fired, exploded

again, its electric web riveting out
from the trunk, the man in its circumference,

flattened, shocked face up,
questioning the sky.

Before the medics wheeled him off,
did he remember in the next county over

the teen dashing through rain,
lightning's long finger tapping her twice,

a parody of the da Vinci painting?
For weeks she was a celebrity.

"He is a fool," the papers said,
"and should have known better."

But what odds we all give and take,
daily loading blank dice into our hopeful palms.

Bad things happen in threes,
but it's twice, the highly unlikely,

that slips in in the middle
and slips us up.

And those of us, the survivors of "bad things,"
of storms blindingly fierce and electric,

even on clear, bright days,
will we continue, with hope

or fear, to look up straight
into whatever warms us?

Section III

39

Given a stack of Scriptures
as tall as I am old, I'd swear
to its untruth, this claim of age
mistaken, misplaced in my life,
certificates switched or censored;
parents and siblings bribed;
the family dog who came much later
a wholly unreliable witness;

a husband and child who swallowed
the lies of birthdays, sang dutifully
as if time and I were really bellowing
into this wind across the precipice
of forty. It's wrong

to fool the mind when the body
can't get enough of the good joke,
when the belly forgets flattery
and unflattens its feminine bulge.
(We'll stay off the subject of breasts
as the back also loves gravity
and tips to-fro, to-fro across this off-key xylophone
of a spine.) But the mind knows—

doesn't it?—the knot looped
the wrong way, the direction tugged
too far south in this tug-of-war
over belief and mathematics.
My whole life I have seen who I am,
where I will be; who better than I
to identify and deny the middle-age
I have, unknowingly, become?

IN THE PEARLE VISION CENTER WAITING ROOM

Here we stare past each other,
focus on blurred prints across the room,
honeymoon spots or monasteries—
we can't tell—rocks and palm trees
merging to greenish-gray.

What we see in the plastic reflection
is ourselves waiting
to see. On the near wall,
rows of Claiborne frames,
fragile octagons. We look

them right in the eye,
pretend to choose what we can't
see the other wearing,
a way of remembering, forgetting,
to find at the bottom

of the chart, below the B F S C A D in fine print,
sacred Scripture, or a love note
from the mysterious admirer who is,
after all, one of us in glasses
and fake mustache

as in the story you read to me now
from the dog-eared magazine
aging on the waiting room table:
*Amnesia Victim Wooed Again by Husband,
Remarried in Grand Ceremony*;

how we see in her forgetting, fragments
of the familiar, the vision to fall

not blindly but clearly again
into that just out-of-sight,
around-the-corner, or in the peripheral

of the everyday, a glimpse of the love-
worn stare; in each glossy the focused eyes
of two-hundred twenty-year
friends toasting their sparkling
again. Her doctors smile and eat cake.

The bride and groom look straight
into the camera at us.

CLYDE PEELING'S REPTILAND

Allenwood, PA

Evenings, they rent
out, wedding reception
guests winding in
and out between glass cages
that reflect back
delight in fearing
its trapped
spectators.

A martini with the Black Mambas,
hors d'oeuvres with the Indian Pythons,
chicken with the unfried
two-toned arrow-poison frogs
and their nervously twitching legs.

At 10:00, the bride rides the Aldabra Tortoise,
her long gown wound around her elbow
or flung wildly down, zig-zagging its trail
in dirt transplanted
from some Pennsylvania farm
where optimistic rodents dream
of gulping pit vipers
whole.

It is slow going.

Metamorphosis is the vow of the hour,
hanging in the ever-changing air
like an overdone toast
mixed with Twisted Sister.

No French-kissing here
in full view of forked tongues
but there's a tense attempt
when the couples' lip rings clink
at each rattle of the wine glass.

It is all the Common Iguana can do
to not smirk when the tattooed groom
tries to smile, line-dancing his way
along Amphibians' Lane.

Soon everyone sips and hisses;
the quietest drunks leave
their skins behind.

Later, the DJ howls outside
the crocodile pit where four-star acoustics
uncoil the sound
to the local penitentiary
and inmates bet
on accidental deaths.

INDELIBLE

> "Jim C., of Cincinnati, Ohio, has a tattooed
> wedding band."
> —from *Romance 101: Lessons in Love*,
> Chapter on Commitment

Before he said, "I do," the groom
had it done, inked himself
a circle of seraphs, sunk
thin swirls into skin that clutched
the bone like a bride
unable to hide a not-slim leg
within a garnished garter.

At the prescribed time,
he handed his love his hand
attached to an arm of Botticellian artwork.

Or maybe his best man,
in from the Bronx, Detroit, or even Boise,
light-skinned proprietor of The Dark Horse,
resourcefully used the only outlet behind the altar
to jab the high-tech indigo ink
succinctly into the fingers held out before a priest
in a Bud-Light T-shirt and collar.

Then this friend etched matching sets
in purples and pinks entwined.
Everyone waited patiently, except the soon-to-be
mother-in-law, who fainted.

But she was revived quickly
and helped when the fuchsia-dyed cake injected,
inconveniently, with badly burnt brandy
was cut in precise slices
and placed on a skin of napkin.

Which is what I ate
the moment I saw your permanent eyes,
a half-heart tattooed so vividly
on each matching lid.

AT THE GYNECOLOGIST'S

Here, what is in will out
in a cup not tipped up
for drinking, or clip-clip
on a dish or slide your insides
spread like jelly. It's a jam
we're in when the lights don't dim
and we've stripped with our lips tight
and our limbs wide
enough to see what's still in
somewhat the same position,
though, if age has her say,
won't be long. Of course,
there's the choice to hold
on tight to the site
where the growth grips
its death-hold wholly
and blooms like a kiss
pricked with poison—or maybe
the striptease is really free
of crossbones and, yes,
it's a baby.

PLEA TO AN EMBRYO

Stay put.
Wait till the apron strings are cut
for you. We'll give
you the car keys,
when you're ready;
let you vroom-vroom across the country
in a properly-inspected, reputable car.

We'll let your budding ears
double as bulletin-boards
for beaded jewelry,
your nose and navel nonnegotiable.

We'll watch as you shave your head
to its baby bareness
and say nothing
through our adult teeth.

Wait,
take your first breath. Think
before you split
into nothingness. You're still

under our roof
and rules. We promise,
we promise, you'll understand
if you're older.

DONATION

Each month he jerks
life into a jar. It is not
romantic. But neither is love
with its same blank walls, shut door,
low voices, others waiting.
Too tired to scream, love comes

routinely, holds its own face
in its hands. Outside
embryonic flakes flutter
toward tongues, an almost taste.
He cannot hunch

enough to shake what replicates:
streets, snow, cells, sorrow. Ice-like
the city prisms what isn't. He watches
the children throw snow,
knows none of them.

FIRST LAYOUT

A page in *Baby Magazine*,
you flip beneath the folds of my belly, or
not-yet a page, a pica-person,
punctuating our breaths with exclamation!

Hallelujah! we sing and Oh, no!
and Look-how-this-snap-of-a-photoshot-
flashes-glossy-with-
us! My love, so proud

of the product, types ferociously
his testosterone history
on the glimmer of you,
film-like and floating
in your development.

I, too, am bursting
with words that say nothing
but Ah!

Oh, little one,
how patiently you pose
with wonder at your prenatal parents,
waiting for us to create
our perfect captions.

TWIN INFANTS AT THE OLAN MILLS PORTRAIT STUDIO

Though identical, they are strikingly
not, the cheeks of one hollowed out
by the girth of the other, as if the sister
embryo sucked portions of flesh
from her unlike clone. The camera will click
them together, give their difference a backdrop
of pink, pretend identical cuteness. There are not
enough photographic tricks for this. The large one
croons and chews on her chubby toes, chuckles just-so;
the other, eyes sunken as a drunk's,
clings to a mother who claims she's "bad." It is easy
to tell them apart, but which,
young woman, will you give to the woods,
to the sad wind on the top of a mountain?

SWIMMING PREGNANT AT THE YWCA

Double buoys, we dip
together, bob, pull in
mouthfuls, push out

rhythms of oxygen. Or,
fat frog and tadpole
in this clear cool of wet,

we breaststroke beginnings.
Beside us, women
in their seventies, stretch

flabby limbs, step up
and down on plastic.
Their waves wash us

cleaner, circle our double
bellies with what
they've already breathed.

On the other side,
two women younger than I,
compare daughters'

applications to college:
what they know, will learn.
I go under, watch

these women's legs move
and move. I cross
their current; surface, repeat.

MARCH 16

You came out
of my slashed belly,
green and gagging, gasping
for the faith of air. We believed
you wouldn't live, that your wing-
shaped lungs wouldn't flutter you far
into prayers stuck trefoil in our throats.
On Saint Patrick's eve, your skin, grey-green
and tainted with everything dark and dead,
revived us of little faith, babes buried
in our own fears, waiting to be
rebirthed in the holy
hope that was you.

AFTERNOON NAP

My daughter dreams breasts, lip-synching lunch.
I am the large one beside her,
a sleepy parenthesis curl for her appetite.
Like a sleepwalker descending stair
after stair with rhythmic certainty,
she munches air convinced of flesh and fluid.
I dream of rest, also fooled.

THE TIME IS MIDNIGHT

My dead father hiccups up the stairs,
down the hall, in my daughter's sleep,
startles her waking, startles me,
with those twins of absence/
presence, staccato air studded
where he isn't, where she is. Which
one of us cries "dada" in the half-light
of street lamps, manmade moons
we howl after as time climbs over
to another date? What we hold
is ourselves holding on,
the language of letting go
untongued in our infant mouths.
I am crying. I am crying.
I am cradling the dear voice
of my child's stirring,
the deep past of my childhood weeping,
rocking all midnights to sleep.

APPROPRIATE

My friend Lucille wears only black and gives away
a shirt, a sweater, a short stretch skirt each time she buys
another piece of fabric. Her etiquette
of funeral apparel: "Wear according to your consciousness
of grief," and so I dress my six-month daughter
in pink to match the absence of loss
she feels at her first funeral: a woman we did not know
who had my name and died the way my father did,
hoping for a heart to make him whole.

The husband, who forgets my name,
says my daughter will break hearts
as she coos and drools on my black dress
that clothes me in tradition if not grief.
Some here wear gray stretch pants,
some white high heels after Labor Day.
I look to see where grief is draped;
my daughter starts to cry. In these stiff pews,
I sway to calm her.

In his gold cope, the priest is speaking
of his baby, who shares the deceased's name
with me. His eldest daughter, Lucy,
lights the candles white and smiles at my child.
I hold my small one tighter at the prayers
and think I hear my father's hopeful voice.

But it is still the priest, reciting
Hopkins' poem to Margaret.
His clean, bald head shines baby-like in candlelight
the way, ten years ago, it must have caught the shadows

of cigarettes in New York coffee houses
as he read poems to cope
with what he saw each city day.

It is clean and rural here. My friend,
now far away in Boston wearing black,
grieves her life. She wants a child and home.
My daughter shares her middle name,
her thick, rich hair that curls above a face
that has my father's color.
I take my daughter home and change our clothes,
something appropriate to the weather.

MONA LISA

My daughter stares at her stare,
stretches her own small lips taut,
hums a moan that roams the length
of the gallery, echoing our own
first encounters. The mystery
is our own minds untrapped
by the tight frame that fences
our lives, by the paradoxical portrait
that frees us: the gasp not escaping
the lady's lips, the epiphany
sparkling my daughter's eyes,
the sad joy that lets her see
all that the world is.

ABSTRACT

After the Jackson Pollock movie
where Ed Harris won't stop jabbing
that paintbrush and voice
into my non-cinematic air,
I want to make something big
and screaming.

My friend says I need a wife for that.
My husband agrees, complains he's one,
but still brings me sandwiches
when I type shut the door,
whispering little words
too small for canvas.

At night, after the children
cry their separation fears,
we watch thrillers on a screen
the size of Pollock's visions,
high-definition substituted for paint.

What can be superimposed on this life
I love and flee from to re-create
the concrete, the already-here,
flat and fading on these walls
big enough for the expressionist,
for me?

GOLDFISH

Pre-election

Two months after
the kindergarten teacher bribed
her first-week class with fins swishing
in a plastic bag, my son still loves the living
surprise that refuses the death
of its predecessors, those already rotting
before their fated slide
down labyrinthian pipes.

"In the back of its jaw are teeth,"
he tells us daily, "small but sharp,"
and he smiles to show his own
just-brushed whites.

At night, I grind mine,
clenching a world
I can't digest.

Together, my son and I pitch
Ping-Pong balls at county carnivals,
winning "friends" that chase
the first Goldie around its glass
encasement. It's why we watch
the way we do, in wonderment
and fear, everywhere and nowhere
to go, the watery wasteland
cloudy with excrement.

And so we wash the make-shift
home weekly, shocked each time
at the cleaned-up view,
man-made but magic in its shine.

When, oblivious, I knick the bowl
against the kitchen spigot, the fish
say nothing, keep swimming
within the fractured globe
that slowly leaks what they need
to breathe. Hours later,
the floor is soaked
with my mistake, the goldfish
somehow still alive
as I breathe deeply,
take in the oxygen-filled air,
my son beside me, scared.

What can fifty dollars buy
if not security? A tank, plastic ferns,
a fantasy castle, a bubbling attachment
to filter out all the necessary waste,
the hum of this new machine
the medicine that lulls me to sleep
peacefully in the postponement
of death.

H. G. WHO?

"I'm going back in the time machine;
I'll be right back," my daughter hollers
from the backyard when it's time
to set the table. I let her go
off into that world of minutes
cartwheeling backwards
and upside down into the oblivion
of imagination I once knew
in that past she's hurtling toward.

I stay where the seconds click
toward pot roast and green beans,
which she'll later leave on her plate,
off to visit the moon
or that strange new solar system
calling to be discovered.

STILL LIFE OF HOUSE IN LATE MARCH

A century old, she knows
how to pose, shutters not even twitching
in natural light as the artist tinkers
with perception, vandalizes the stark air
with voyeurism. She is naked
of snow, leaves, flowers
but beautiful in her simple stance
among curved hills.

Maybe her weathered
boards will creak onto canvas
or a swallow peep through the brushstrokes
where a nest clogs a slanting chimney.
She is not saying, obedient
to the solemn man now sketching
wrinkles across her face,
re-constructing shadows
of memory,

while beyond his vision,
she daydreams of us
who are watching inside,
forever waiting to see
what she will tell of our lives still
moving and moving.

SETTLED

It's true, we promised this town and state
we wouldn't bother them, wouldn't dig
ourselves into their coal-veined soil,
into their local rituals and healings.
Burrs in their Pennsylvania wind,
we'd drift, stick at most a year
in these hills four hours from everywhere
flashing, bright, and familiar.

Now, even the weeds call us liars
as we tug their choking gaze
from around our mortgaged home,
comprehend the complexity of roots
suddenly shooting in directions
unpredictable, but as stable
as these rough floorboards
across which we walk nightly
to kiss asleep the children
born surprisingly in this small town
where we wake
each morning to each other.

All of our other lives
are planted deep:
those hacked down,
those waiting to sprout
in some future that will not grow
though watered with fervor.
Still, we look out these streaked windows
and see who we are.

And now, even I,
who hold place as close as Scripture,
am starting to believe.

AFTER HAVING CHILDREN, WE REINTRODUCE OURSELVES TO BICYCLES

This is the teeter-totter
of childhood carelessly forgotten.
Only fear remembers to grip.

Some other self weighs air and metal,
tightropes the balance.

The main rule is to move
and we tongue-lash memory mercilessly
for hesitations.

Misshapen Y of a frame—
your arms stretching up—
pole-body that threatens castration,
we foolishly adore you.

For freedom,
we tense our bodies,
hover over leather
triangles that love too much
our sticky bottoms.

Bent-double,
almost sniffing asphalt,
we'll let your spinning fins propel us;
push to pursue
what's just beyond
sight and folly.

Behind us, our children's tandem
laughter pedals smoothly,
speeding us so easily
after happily.

A. M. : INSIDE AND OUT

Here is the landscape of my son,
prying open the horizon with his grin;
of my daughter, trying to crack the sun
with her large laughter.

What of the clock that clucks, "No, no, no"?
They've flushed it down the commode
with all the toilet-training paraphernalia
until it backs up in the pipes,
bulges beautifully into the hills
that belch so early, "Hello, hello, good morning."

Of course, we must answer,
must gather up the dew and daffodils
in our nightshirts, comb our hair through
with the larks' incessant trill,
our two small ones trailing after us
into the wonderfully, brightening world.

www.ingramcontent.com/pod-product-compliance
Lightning Source LLC
Chambersburg PA
CBHW070513090426
42735CB00012B/2767